My Council Tax Stance

PAUL PATTERSON

Copyright © 2016 Paul Patterson

All rights reserved.

DEDICATION

This book is dedicated to all those fighting the worms

CONTENTS

	Introduction	1
1	Arms Investment	3
2	Lawful Reason or Withholding Council Tax	12
3	The Summons & Liability Order	18
4	Letters To & From The Magistrates' Court	43
5	Bridget Prentice's Report To Parliament	63
6	Local Government Act 1888	72
7	Ministry Of Justice	75
8	Cornwall Council's Enforcement Agents Policy	82
9	Removal Of Implied Rights	87

| 10 | Letter To My MP Sheryll Murray | 96 |
| 11 | Poor law Civil Jurisdiction | 104 |

INTRODUCTION

This all started in January 2016 when my son Jay started to tell me how the council were investing in arms companies, if that wasn't immoral enough, it came apparent that the council are deceiving people who have fallen into arrears with their council tax. They are deceiving them in the summons they are sending out to them. The summons are nothing more than an invitation to the councils place of business, a room in the magistrates court, nothing to do with the magistrates, just a way of putting fear into you. Hundreds of people all summons to appear at Bodmin Magistrates Court on a Thursday afternoon at 1.30pm.

A council officer will be waiting to usher you

into their place of business, get you into agreeing to paying by instalment and that way excepting liability without even seeing a magistrate.

The following information is purely based on my experiences over the last twelve months. Anyone wishing to use the following information does so, in the full knowledge that they take the full responsibility for their actions.

I ask reader's to not believe what they read, until they do their own research. Research all the links, the use of any or all information that follows implies the reader's acceptance of this disclaimer.

CHAPTER 1

ARMS INVESTMENT

With a little research I found that Cornwall Council for some years have been investing money in arms companies.

Cornwall Council has said:

"The overriding concern of the council's pension fund is to provide a sound financial return for thousands of people reliant on the pension in Cornwall. The council aims to keep a balanced portfolio of investments and has a publicly available Statement of Investment Principles, which is rigidly adhered to. A local authority pension fund cannot, however, decide unilaterally not to invest in areas such as the arms industry if doing so would impact on the overall investment return achieved."

So it seems they're not concerned that cluster bombs are being dropped on civilians and kids.

Through the Freedom of Information Act 2000 I asked Cornwall Council, "Can you tell me the names of the arms companies the Council have investment in, and how much investment is in these companies."

The council replied with, "I can confirm that the Council has a nil investment in arms companies."

Kind regards

Alison Crawford

Business Support Officer

Strategy and Engagement

Customer Support Services

Cornwall Council

To this I replied,

"If Cornwall Council have now stopped investing in arms, weapon companies, could you please tell me what year the council stopped investing in weapon companies. I have just found that Cornwall Pension Fund invested in BAE Systems £5,446,630 in 2007."

BAE Systems, is the UK's largest arms company.

Response:

The Council does not hold any shares in these companies

The position on BAE Systems was fully sold

out of in July 12.

Information provided by: Business Planning and Development Service

Date of response: 10th November 2016

So I replied with,

"Am I not correct in saying, Cornwall County Council have 21.9% invested with a company called Newton Fund Managers, who are a subsiduary of Bank of New York Mellon, and if you look into Bank of New York Mellon you find quotes like this:-"A Global Report on the Financing of Nuclear Weapons Producers'. The report, viewed by Ethical Consumer in December 2013, stated that BNY Mellon currently had an estimated USD 4,264.99 million invested or available for the nuclear weapon producers identified in the report. It was reported that BNY Mellon had given bank loans to Alliant Techsystems, Bechtel, Boeing, General Dynamics, Honeywell International, Northrop Grumman,

Rockwell Collins and SAIC. It was stated that the company held shares in Aecom, Alliant Techsystems, Babcock & Wilcox, Boeing, Fluor, GenCorp, General Dynamics, Honeywell International."

The council replied with, "At the following link you will find Newton's ESG policy on our website
https://www.cornwall.gov.uk/media/3626943/Newton-ri_policies_and_procedures.pdf

Please see our most recent Annual Report which contains the principles by which we abide, our Statement of Investment Principles details how we invest
https://www.cornwall.gov.uk/media/22161482/cornwall-pension-fund-report-2015-16-final.pdf

Newton Investment Managers are a fund manager, who manage portfolios. Newton Investment Managers manages a global equity portfolio for the Cornwall Pension Fund.

Please also see the below link, which gives legal guidance into how pension funds should invest, a summary is, "The administering authority's power of investment must be exercised for investment purposes, and not for any wider purposes" and "Investment decisions must therefore be directed towards achieving a wide variety of suitable investments, and to what is best for the financial position of the fund (balancing risk and return in the normal way)."

http://www.pensionfundsonline.co.uk/content/pension-funds-insider/legal/lgps-funds-receive-legal-advice-about-tobacco-divestment/1355

Kind regards

Alison Crawford

Business Support Officer

Strategy and Engagement

Customer Support Services

Cornwall Council

Cornwall Pension Fund Annual Report 2014 – 15 shows that on 31st March 2015 the council had 20.4% of their funds in Newton Investment Managers.

"Cornwall county council have investment in Newton Fund Managers one of nine UK financial institutions providing financial services including loans, shares and bonds to companies that produce cluster bombs amounting to £1.1 billion."

Cluster bombs are illegal weapons banned by the 2008 Convention on Cluster Munitions. The UK has ratified the Convention but has not yet made it explicit through legislation that British financial institutions are prohibited from investing in the production of cluster bombs.

In 2009 in a Ministerial statement the government announced that the provision of funds directly contributing to the manufacture of cluster bombs would become illegal and announced that it planned to work with the financial industry and non-governmental organisations to promote a voluntary code of conduct to prevent indirect financing – but no progress has been made to date.

Some key findings of the report "World-wide Investments in Cluster Munitions: a Shared Responsibility" produced by IKV Pax Christi which details the scale of investment in the producers of this deadly weapon by banks, pension funds and other financial institutions around the world:

The report finds that 139 financial institutions world-wide are investing over US$24 billion (£15 billion) in companies producing cluster munitions.

Nine UK financial institutions are providing financial services including loans, shares and bonds to companies that produce cluster bombs amounting to £1.1 billion, these include: Royal Bank of Scotland, Aberdeen Asset Management, Invesco, Newton Investment Management. Old Mutual, Prudential, Schroders Investment

Management, Standard Life, Veritas Asset Management

Newton Investment Managers are a fund manager, who manages portfolios. Newton Investment Managers manages a global equity portfolio for the Cornwall Pension Fund.

On 19th December 2016 the BBC reported that, Michael Fallon confirms UK-made cluster bombs were being used in Yemen.

Defence Secretary Michael Fallon said Saudi Arabia had confirmed munitions bought from the UK in the 1980s had been dropped.

Since 2010 it has been illegal under British law to supply the bombs, which put civilians at risk by releasing small bomblets over a wide area.

In a statement to MPs, Mr Fallon said the UK had not supplied any cluster bombs to Saudi Arabia since 1989.

CHAPTER 2

LAWFUL REASON FOR WITHHOLDING COUNCIL TAX

Section 15 & 17 of The 2000 Terrorism Act & Section 51 and 52 International Criminal Court Act 2001 gives us all a lawful reason to withhold our council tax.

Under Section 13A of the Local Government Finance Act 1992 a billing authority has power to reduce amount of tax payable

(1)Where a person is liable to pay council tax in respect of any chargeable dwelling and any day, the billing authority for the area in which the dwelling is situated may reduce the amount which he is liable to pay as respects the dwelling and the day to such extent as it thinks fit.

(2)The power under subsection (1) above includes power to reduce an amount to nil.

(3)The power under subsection (1) may be exercised in relation to particular cases or by determining a class of case in which liability is to be reduced to an extent provided by the determination.

http://www.legislation.gov.uk/ukpga/1992/14/section/13A

Sections 15 and 17 of the Terrorism Act 2000:

Under the Terrorism Act 2000

15 Fund-raising.

(1)A person commits an offence if he—

(a)invites another to provide money or other property, and

(b)intends that it should be used, or has reasonable cause to suspect that it may be used, for the purposes of terrorism.

(2)A person commits an offence if he—

(a)receives money or other property, and

(b)intends that it should be used, or has reasonable cause to suspect that it may be used, for the purposes of terrorism.

(3)A person commits an offence if he—

(a)provides money or other property, and

(b)knows or has reasonable cause to suspect that it will or may be used for the purposes of terrorism.

(4)In this section a reference to the provision of money or other property is a reference to its being given, lent or otherwise made available, whether or not for consideration.

17 Funding arrangements.

A person commits an offence if—

(a)he enters into or becomes concerned in an arrangement as a result of which money or other property is made available or is to be made available to another, and

(b)he knows or has reasonable cause to

suspect that it will or may be used for the purposes of terrorism. Source for above information
http://www.legislation.gov.uk/ukpga/2000/11/introduction

Section 51 and 52 International Criminal Court Act 2001.

51 Genocide, crimes against humanity and war crimes

(1)It is an offence against the law of England and Wales for a person to commit genocide, a crime against humanity or a war crime.

(2)This section applies to acts committed—

(a)in England or Wales, or

(b)outside the United Kingdom by a United Kingdom national, a United Kingdom resident or a person subject to UK service jurisdiction.

52 Conduct ancillary to genocide, etc. committed outside jurisdiction.

(1)It is an offence against the law of England and Wales for a person to engage in conduct ancillary to an act to which this section applies.

(2)This section applies to an act that if committed in England or Wales would constitute—

(a)an offence under section 51 (genocide, crime against humanity or war crime), or

(b)an offence under this section,

but which, being committed (or intended to be committed) outside England and Wales, does not constitute such an offence.

(3)The reference in subsection (1) to conduct ancillary to such an act is to conduct that would constitute an ancillary offence in relation to that act if the act were committed in England or Wales.

(4)This section applies where the conduct in question consists of or includes an act committed—

(a)in England or Wales, or

(b)outside the United Kingdom.

http://www.legislation.gov.uk/ukpga/2001/1

7/section/51

The Rome Statute of the International Criminal Court – summary of article 25.3 (c)

A person, who aids, abets or assists in the commission of a crime of genocide, a crime against humanity or a war crime, including providing the means for its commission, shall be criminally responsible and liable for punishment.

CHAPTER 3

THE SUMMONS & LIABILITY ORDER

This process is determined by The Council Tax (Administration and Enforcement) 1992 Regulations 33 - 36 in particular.

http://www.legislation.gov.uk/uksi/1992/613/regulation/33/madeRegulations

Application for liability order
34.—(1) If an amount which has fallen due under regulation 23(3) or (4) is wholly or partly unpaid, or (in a case where a final notice is required under regulation 33) the amount stated in the final notice is wholly or partly unpaid at the expiry of the period of 7 days

beginning with the day on which the notice was issued, the billing authority may, in accordance with paragraph (2), apply to a magistrates' court for an order against the person by whom it is payable.

(2) The application is to be instituted by making complaint to a justice of the peace, and requesting the issue of a summons directed to that person to appear before the court to show why he has not paid the sum which is outstanding.

(6) The court shall make the order if it is satisfied that the sum has become payable by the defendant and has not been paid.

35.—(1) A single liability order may deal with one person and one such amount (or aggregate amount) as is mentioned in regulation 34(7) and (8) (in which case the order shall be in the form specified as Form A in Schedule 2, or a form to the like effect), or, if the court thinks fit, may deal with more than one person and more than one such amount (in which case the order shall be in the form specified as Form B in that Schedule, or a form to the like effect).

(2) A summons issued under regulation 34(2) may be served on a person—

(a) by delivering it to him, or

(b) by leaving it at his usual or last known place of abode, or in the case of a company, at its registered office, or

(c) by sending it by post to him at his usual or last known place of abode, or in the case of a company, to its registered office, or

(d) by leaving it at, or by sending it by post to him at, an address given by the person as an address at which service of the summons will be accepted.

(3) The amount in respect of which a liability order is made is enforceable in accordance with this Part; and accordingly for the purposes of any of the provisions of Part III of the Magistrates' Courts Act 1980 (satisfaction and enforcement) it is not to be treated as a sum adjudged to be paid by order of the court.

Duties of debtors subject to liability order

36.—(1) Where a liability order has been made, the debtor against whom it was made shall, during such time as the amount in respect of which the order was made remains wholly or partly unpaid, be under a duty to supply relevant information to the billing authority on whose application it was made.

(2) For the purposes of paragraph (1), relevant information is such information as fulfils the following conditions—

(a) it is in the debtor's possession or control;

(b) the billing authority requests him by notice given in writing to supply it; and

(c) it falls within paragraph (3).

(3) Information falls within this paragraph if it is specifed in the notice mentioned in paragraph (2)(b) and it falls within one or more of the following descriptions—

(a) information as to the name and address of an employer of the debtor;

(b) information as to earnings or

expected earnings of the debtor;

(c)information as to deductions and expected deductions from such earnings in respect of the matters referred to in paragraphs (a) to (c) of the definition of "net earnings" in regulation 32 or attachment of earnings orders made under this Part, the Attachment of Earnings Act 1971(1) or the Child Support Act 1991(2);

(d) information as to the debtor's work or identity number in an employment, or such other information as will enable an employer of the debtor to identify him;

(e) information as to sources of income of the debtor other than an employer of his;

(f) information as to whether another person is jointly and severally liable with the debtor for the whole or any part of the amount in respect of which the order was made.

(4) Information is to be supplied within 14 days of the day on which the request is made.

(3) The amount in respect of which a liability order is made is enforceable in accordance with this Part; and accordingly for the purposes of any of the provisions of Part III of the Magistrates' Courts Act 1980 (satisfaction and enforcement) **it is not to be treated as a sum adjudged to be paid by order of the court.**

The magistrates and council don't seem to realise that The Council Tax (Administration and Enforcement) 1992 Regulations conflict with case law and THE SUPREME COURT & EUROPEAN COURT OF HUMAN RIGHTS.

http://hudoc.echr.coe.int/eng#{"itemid":["001-68421"]}

http://www.bailii.org/ew/cases/EWCA/Civ/2004/1689.html

http://www.bailii.org/ew/cases/EWHC/Admin/2002/2467.html

"I find it very surprising that the only document with a court stamp (under xiii) is not produced by the court, but is created automatically by the local authority's software, even though the local authority is a party to the proceedings. (The example before us adds, under the court stamp, the words "Justice of the Peace for the area aforesaid (or by order of the Court Clerk of the Court)". The intended significance of these words is not clear to me.) This document apparently is used only for the purpose of confirming to the bailiff that he has power to act. However, for that purpose the rules require no more than "the written authorisation of the authority" (Non-domestic Rating (Collection and Enforcement) (Local Lists) Regulations 1989 r.14(5)). It seems both unnecessary, and wrong in principle, for it to be presented as though it had been stamped by the court. Nothing turns on this point in the present case, and we have not heard any submissions about it, but it seems to me an aspect of the procedure which merits reconsideration." Lord Justice Waller THE SUPREME COURT.

"(i) The decision of the justices that the applicant had culpably neglected to pay her community charge without having conducted a proper inquiry into her circumstances as of the time that the liability became due was unlawful, see R. v. Leeds Justices ex parte Kennett [1996] RVR 53.

http://hudoc.echr.coe.int/eng#{"itemid":["001-68421"]}

The magistrates' never conducted an inquiry into circumstances at liability hearings, they don't have the authority under The Council

Tax (Administration and Enforcement) 1992 Regulations.

Its clear from the above regulations that the magistrates court make/issue the order, nowhere in these regulations does it state that the magistrates court can give authority for the council to issue and print the orders on their own computer software. You'll find that the council keeps all the records, when contacting the court on council tax issues you are told, 'We don't keep records of council tax hearing.'

Applications for liability orders to the magistrates' court are presented to the magistrates in bulk, hearings with hundreds of names listed. There is no way that due process can be followed in this fashion.

Bulk listing may comply with The Council Tax (Administration and Enforcement) 1992 Regulations, but they don't comply with the magistrates judicial functions. So the council doesn't only have The Council Tax (Administration and Enforcement) 1992 regulations to comply with, in using the Magistrates Court, the court have their own rules and regulations to comply with.

Lord Widgery C.J, stated, regarding the following case.

Regina v. Brentford Justices, Ex parte Catlin [1975]

"It must however be remembered that before a summons or warrant is issued the information must be laid before a magistrate and he must go through the judicial exercise of deciding whether a summons or warrant ought to be issued or not. **If a magistrate authorises the issue of a summons without having applied his mind to the information then he is guilty of dereliction of** duty and if in any particular justices' clerk's office a practice goes on of summonses being issued without information being laid before the magistrate at all, then a very serious instance of maladministration arises which should have the attention of the authorities without delay."

"A decision by magistrates whether to issue a summons pursuant to information laid involves the exercise of a judicial function, and is not merely administrative."

So once I'd had the final demands from the council, sometime later I received the summons.

As you now know the summons doesn't come from the magistrate's court, the council has their own computer software, which generates the summons and liability orders. The above summons has an electronic signature under it the words, Clerk to the Justices. The Magistrates court and council are acting unlawfully.

The Magistrates' Courts Rules 1981 states:

Summons

Form of Summons

98. -(1) A summons shall be signed by the justice issuing it or state his name and be authenticated by the signature of the clerk of magistrates court.

We only ever get a summons with electronic signature of the clerk to the justices, never any name stated.

We need to wonder why these summons and liability orders are not authenticated by a printed name and court seal. If its correct that the magistrates court do and have authority to allow the council to use software to print their own summons and liability orders, why don't the court allow the council to use court seal and printed name of signature?

I asked this question to the magistrates' court, they replied with the following:

Subject: Summons

Dear Mr Patterson

We have sent your email to the legal advisers, who have responded with the following:

The rules permit facsimile signatures to be

used. The act of the authorisation of the issue of the summons is undertaken by a person delegated with that authority such as a legal adviser and Mr Smith has given permission for his signature to be used.

Yours faithfully

 Mrs Yelland

Administration Officer

So you can see with the above comments from the courts legal advisers they are not following the Magistrates Court Rules 1981. Yes, it is correct that an electronic signature can be used, but it must also be accompanied by a printed name. The reason for this is because the court didn't issue the summons, it was issued by the council. The court will have no record of the council tax summons, as you will see later.

As you can see, the magistrates' court and council have this cosy relationship with no rules, making it impossible for you to get a fair hearing if you are daft enough to except the councils invitation to THEIR hearing, in a room at the magistrates court. You have to understand that these hearings are not HMCTS hearings and no CIVIL PROCEDURE RULES applies. If council tax hearing were genuine HMCTS hearing CPR would have to apply.

If you attend your summons hearing, which I advise you not to, you will find a council officer try to usher you into a side room to agree to monthly payments and in that way accepting liability. You must insist on seeing the magistrates you must hold your ground and insist on the magistrates answering the following questions before any hearing take place. By doing this you will most certainly stop the hearing taking place:

'Is this a judicial or administrative procedure? & Is this a HMCTS court hearing? Do the Civil Procedure Rules apply to the hearing? If not, which rules do apply?' You need to ask the names of the magistrates and ask are they on their oath.

'The Anonymous JP'." 'Regina v Felixstowe'

"The Court is required to provide this information to the parties in the case, and any others having an interest in the case (i.e. witnesses etc.) by virtue of the judgement in the case 'Regina v Felixstowe' justices ex parte Leigh and another, Queens bench division c 1984/5. Held by Lord Justice Watson that :- There is a right to know who sits in judgement, and denial of that right is unlawful, unwarranted and inimical to the proper administration of justice, further that there is no such person known to Law as 'the anonymous JP'."

We hear it said that Liability Orders are not being recorded in the prescribed form and do not exist in writing. The Council Tax (Administration and Enforcement) (Amendment) (No. 2) (England) Regulations 2003, regulation 3 of, removed the requirement for orders to be in a specified form. It seems it did not abolish the power to make the orders. It puzzles me why they would want to removed the prescribed form other than the magistrates had never had the authority to issue the LO. Never the less, if it comes from a magistrates' court it should comply with The Magistrates court Rules 1982 which it doesn't.

Here is Tim Smith, Justices' Clerk for Devon, Cornwall and Dorset's explanation:

The order can be set out in a format which the court deems satisfactory - but it will need to include certain basic information such as the name of the person against whom it was made, when it was made and in what amount. It should specify the court which made the order, but does not require a court seal.

The formal order is made by the court, at a hearing in a courtroom open to the public, but the general practice around the country is for the local authority to produce the order after the court has made it.

Is a liability order an ORDER or a STATEMENT?

Well I received my first liability order on 08.04.2016. So I wrote two emails both the same, one to Cornwall Council as a FOI the other to the court.

To: Freedom of Information Mail

Subject: Freedom of Information request -

MY COUNCIL TAX STANCE

What is a liability order?

Dear Cornwall Council,

1. Can you clarify the following which is stated on your web site. "A. Liability order is a statement from the Magistrates Court that you owe an amount of Council Tax and costs. It gives the Council additional powers to enforce the debt."

2. Is a liability order an ORDER or a STATEMENT?

3. If the liability order is an ORDER from the court, doe it not have a court seal on because the order is not issued in a HMCTS court?

4. Is the liability order issued in a HMCTS court where CPR applies?

5. Paper form Liability orders for council tax were revoked in 2003. How are records now kept of liability orders issued?

Yours faithfully,

Paul Patterson

Dear Mr Patterson,

I am writing in response to your email dated the 11 July 2016, sent to the freedom of information request team.

I can confirm the information you have requested can be provided as a normal request for service, as follows:

Can you clarify the following which is stated on your web site. "A. Liability order is a statement from the Magistrates Court that you owe an amount of Council Tax and costs. It gives the Council additional powers to enforce the debt."

1. Is a liability order an ORDER or a STATEMENT?

If the court is satisfied that the sum in question has become payable by the defendant and has not been paid, then it is required to make a liability order in respect of an amount equal to the aggregate of the sum payable and the costs reasonably incurred by the applicant in obtaining the order. The liability order is a statement from the Magistrates Court, as it will report the amount payable including costs.

2.If the liability order is an ORDER from the court, does it not have a court seal on because the order is not issued in a HMCT court?

There is no require for a court seal in accordance with The Council Tax (Administration and Enforcement) Regulations 1992.

3. Is the liability order issued in a HMCT court where CPR applies?

Any such application for a council tax liability

order will be dealt with by the Magistrates court.

Council tax summonses and liability orders are issued in accordance with Council Tax (Administration and Enforcement) Regulations 1992 and Magistrates Courts Act 1980.

4. Paper form Liability orders for council tax were revoked in 2003. How are records now kept of liability orders issued?

All liability orders granted are stored electronically on the council's document management system.

We are committed to dealing with all requests fairly and impartially. However as previously advised, if you continue to contact the Council in such a manner, it is possible that we would refrain from issuing a response to your queries with regards to the recovery action taken against you, in accordance with our Unreasonable Customer Behaviour Policy, which I have previously supplied.

Yours sincerely

Mrs Liza Johnson

Technical Officer Revenues

Communities and Organisational Development

So you can see what happens when they realise that you're on to them, when you catch them out with their unlawful actions in the recovery of council tax.

"If you continue to contact the Council in such a manner, it is possible that we would refrain from issuing a response to your queries with regards to the recovery action taken against you, in accordance with our Unreasonable Customer Behaviour Policy, which I have previously supplied."

I sent the same letter to the magistrates'

court and here is the reply from Tim Smith, Clerk to the justices:

He still didn't answer the question, "WHY" IS THERE NO COURT SEAL ON THE ORDER. Instead he replied "But does not require a court seal." Tell me Tim Smith WHY it doesn't require a court seal?

Dear Mr Patterson,

The order can be set out in a format which the court deems satisfactory - but it will need to include certain basic information such as the name of the person against whom it was made, when it was made and in what amount. It should specify the court which made the order, but does not require a court seal.

The formal order is made by the court, at a hearing in a courtroom open to the public, but the general practice around the country is for the local authority to produce the order after the court has made it.

Yours sincerely

Tim Smith

Tim Smith, Justices' Clerk for Devon, Cornwall and Dorset

Her Majesty's Courts & Tribunals Service

Plymouth Magistrates' Court, St Andrew Street, Plymouth, PL1 2DP

'but the general practice around the country is for the local authority to produce the order after the court has made it.'

'It should specify the court which made the order, but does not require a court seal.'

Nowhere in the Magistrates Courts Rules 1981 or The Council Tax (Administration and Enforcement) Regulations 1992 does it state that the council can produce the order the court has made.

Halsbury's Law on Administrative Courts

1. All Administrative Courts are UNLAWFUl.

2. Administrative Law is nothing more than an arrangement between the Executive and the Judiciary.

"The Law is absolutely clear on this subject. There is no authority for Administrative Courts in the country, and no Act could be passed to legitimise them."

Conclusion: No Fines or Seizures of Property before conviction in a Court of Law (must have a jury) are illegal and banned. Bill of Rights.

The European Court of Human Rights (Fourth Section), sitting on 21 October 2003

http://caselaw.echr.globe24h.com/0/0/united-kingdom/2003/10/21/lloyd-and-44-others-v-the-united-kingdom-23523-29798-96.shtml

B. Relevant domestic law

2. Judicial review

According to Halsbury's Laws of England, Fourth Edition, Volume 1(1) at paragraph 59:

"Judicial review is the process by which the High Court exercises its supervisory jurisdiction over the proceedings and decisions of inferior courts, tribunals and other bodies or persons who carry out quasi-judicial functions or who are charged with the performance of public acts and duties ...

Judicial review is concerned with reviewing not the merits of the decision in respect of which the application for judicial review is made, but the decision

making process itself ...

The duty of the court is to confine itself to the question of legality. Its concern is with whether a decision making authority exceeded its powers, committed an error of law, committed a breach of the rules of natural justice, reached a decision which no reasonable tribunal could have reached or abused its powers.

CHAPTER 4

LETTERS TO & FROM THE MAGISTRATES' COURT

To stop all this stress and hassle I completely ignored the summons and then waited for the council to inform me that the magistrates' court had made a liability order against me. Then I emailed the magistrates' court the following:

To: cornwall-admin

Subject: summonses, warrants or court orders.

Good day,

I'm writing to ask if there are any summonses, warrants or court orders of any description in my name, PAUL PATTERSON date birth 17/10/1956

Which they replied:

Good Afternoon,

Thankyou for your e-mail.

I have searched our system and can confirm that there is currently no active or archived cases for you in the Devon and Cornwall area.

Please note this is only for the Devon and Cornwall Area.

Kind Regards

MY COUNCIL TAX STANCE

Mrs Paula Gilks

Court Support Officer

Cornwall Magistrates' Court

The Law Courts

Launceston Road

Bodmin

PL31 2AL

After a week or so I replied with:

To: cornwall-admin

Subject: Re: summonses, warrants or court orders.

Hi Paula,

The search was for COUNCIL TAX LIABILITY ORDER hearings. I'm requesting a Certified copy of the liability Order and the court record/extract for the two days 8th April 2016 & 5th August 2016 in relation to my hearings.

Kind Regards

Paul Patterson.

Then I got their reply which proves the magistrates court are not following due process or even keeping court records of council tax hearing, because they don't have

MY COUNCIL TAX STANCE

to as the hearing are not HMCTS hearing, but as I have already stated, they are council hearings.

Hello

As your request is concerning council tax liability orders, I have referred your query to the Cornwall Council Legal Dept.

Regards

Mr Rutherford

Administration Officer

Cornwall Magistrates' Court

The Law Courts

Launceston Road

Bodmin, Cornwall

PL31 2AL

You have to laugh, as only twenty minutes

later I received this email, once again from Mr. Rutherford:

Hello

As mentioned in my previous email, your query was passed onto the Cornwall Council. So they can search their records could you supply more detail of the cases in question, such as the addresses you were summonsed for?

Regards

Mr Rutherford

Administration Officer

Cornwall Magistrates' Court

The Law Courts

Launceston Road

Bodmin, Cornwall

PL31 2AL

To: cornwall-admin

Subject: Re: summonses, warrants or court orders.

Hello,

My query was passed onto Cornwall Council so they can search their records? If I have any COURT orders against me, the Magistrates Court will hold them. I'm not interested in any COUNCIL ORDERS. What's this relationship the court has with the council? How can anyone have a fair hearing when the courts have this cosy relationship with the council. If the court hearings are HMCTS hearings they have to follow due process. If there was a court hearing the court will hold the records, never mind this, we have passed your query onto Cornwall Council to search their records. So you are telling me the court have no records and council tax hearing are none HMCTS & there are no CPR rules, and these are council hearings and not COURT HEARINGS?

They must realise by now I have them cornered, anyway they replied with the following:

Good Morning,

Thank you for your e-mail.

I apologise for the previous e-mail that was sent to you. Please let me provide you with more background and explain the court process in regards council tax liability orders.

The Cornwall Council initially send a schedule of names to the court to apply for multiple liability orders. Once the schedule is checked and authorised by the courts legal team the council generate the summonses and send them out to the respective council tax defaulters.

On the date of the hearing the council attend the court and the court go through the schedule and either grant, refuse or adjourn each application as they see fit.

The court do not enter each application for a liability order on our system, the court input the schedule as one case but for multiple liability orders.

The Cornwall Council do their own administration and after the court hearing the Council generate the liability orders that the court has granted.

This is why the court has referred your e-mail to the council as we would not be able to search on our system for individual liability orders.

It would help speed up your query if you could provide us with the addresses that you think you may have been summonsed for council tax so that the council can check their records.

I hope this answers your query

Kind regards

Mrs Paula Gilks

Court Support Officer

Cornwall Magistrates' Court

The Law Courts

Launceston Road

Bodmin

PL31 2AL

Next day I received this email:

Dear Sir,

Thank you for your request regarding liability order proceedings.

MY COUNCIL TAX STANCE

I have asked Paula Gilks, our support officer, to handle your inquiry and to inform you of any decision that may have been made on the said dates.

May I also inform you that there may be a cost involved in this process.

If you are at all considering taking independent legal advice, it may be in your best interests to do so sooner rather than later as an appeal will involve a specific time frame.

Yours faithfully

Paul Miles

Legal Adviser

So I replied to Paula Gilks with:

To: cornwall-admin

Subject: Re: summonses, warrants or court orders.

Hi Paula,

You state, "The Cornwall Council initially send a schedule of names to the court to apply for multiple liability orders. Once the schedule is checked and authorised by the courts legal team." Please can you send me a copy of the original complaint - or list with my name on it...Please give me the names or name of persons involved with 'Checking and Authorising' these complaints.

Paul Patterson.

All the correspondences were emails. So, week later I received the following:

Good Morning,

MY COUNCIL TAX STANCE

Sorry for the delay in my response.

I have searched the council tax schedules for the dates you mentioned and your name has appeared on both of those schedules. Please find attached the schedules from the Council tax courts held at Cornwall Magistrates' on the 8 April 2016 and the 5 August 2016 when these liability orders where granted.

The schedules where checked and authorised by the following legal advisors:

Raul Demenzes for the 8 April 2016

Ivan Hancocks for the 5 August 2016

Kind Regards

Mrs Paula Gilks

Court Support Officer

Cornwall Magistrates' Court

The Law Courts

Launceston Road

Bodmin

PL31 2AL

'Sorry for the delay.' Was most probably because she was colluding with the council.'

I emailed back:

To: cornwall-admin

Subject: Re: summonses, warrants or court orders

Good day,

The council sent me the schedules you have sent me some months ago, the schedule dated 8th April 2016 page 4 is not signed by Raul Demenzes as is the one you have sent me.

To this I received the following:

Good Afternoon,

Thankyou for your e-mail.

The legal advisor who sat on both Council tax court hearings where the liability orders where granted was actually Renee Gallin. However in your previous e-mail you did ask me for the names of the legal advisors who checked and authorised the schedules before the summons to court are issued by the council? i am sorry if i have misunderstood your request.

Can I ask what it is you actually want the court to provide?

Can I also ask why you are requesting the information as I may be able to understand better what details I can give you to satisfy your query.

Kind Regards

Mrs Paula Gilks

Court Support Officer

Cornwall Magistrates' Court

The Law Courts

Launceston Road

Bodmin

PL31 2AL

Subject: Re: summonses, warrants or court orders

Paula,

Can you tell me why the liability orders are signed TIM SMITH clerk to the justices if it was RENEE GALLIN who sat on both council tax hearing where liability orders were granted?

Magistrates final email:

Good Afternoon

Your emails were looked at by our Legal Team who advise:

"The process for liability orders in Council Tax is well established and relatively simple.

Liability orders are sought by the Council. They submit a complaint list to the court requesting authority to issue a summons.

The court authorised the Council to issue the summons. The Council issued the summons.

The hearing took place before a bench of

magistrates on the return date for the summons. That court granted orders and the Chairman of that bench signed the revised list of orders.

It is revised because some applications are withdrawn, some are paid and often some are adjourned.

The process is determined by the regulations. I believe this query relates to a liability order for Council Tax hence the Council Tax (Admin and Enforcement) Regulations 1992 apply, Regulations 33 - 36 in particular.

The process therefore has been in place for 24 years and to my knowledge many years before that prior to the inception of Council Tax. The process has correctly been followed in this case!

The court has given a detailed response to each of the requests so far but the court considers this to be an end to the correspondence on this matter.

Paul Kinsley,

Legal Adviser"

Yours sincerely

Miss Z Jones

Administration Officer

Cornwall Magistrates' Court, Bodmin PL31 2AL

Can not find anywhere in the Council Tax (Admin and Enforcement) Regulations 1992 where it states court can authorise the Council to issue the summons and liability order.
<u>http://www.legislation.gov.uk/uksi/1992/613/regulation/36/made</u>

When did the magistrate give judicial consideration to each and every complaint as lawfully required.

So here we go again, like the council, once they see that you have rumbled them in their unlawful game they state, "The court considers this to be an end to the correspondence on this matter."

CHAPTER 5

BRIDGET PRENTICE'S REPORT TO PARLIAMENT

In 2009 the then Parliamentary undersecretary of State for Justice Bridget Prentice reported to the house that the magistrates courts were not following due process in their handling of council tax hearings. Below is the report to parliament:

Investigations by HMCS

JUSTICE

Council Tax Enforcement (Magistrates Courts)

The Parliamentary Under-Secretary of State for Justice (Bridget Prentice): Local authorities use the magistrates courts to enforce non-payment of council tax. This process begins with an application (called a "complaint") for the court to issue a summons informing the individual that the local authority is seeking unpaid council tax and asking the individual to attend court if they wish to challenge the court making a liability order for that amount. The issue of a summons for non-payment of council tax or non-domestic rates must be authorised by a justice of the peace or legal adviser with delegated powers from a justices' clerk. Fees are chargeable and the decision of the court at the hearing must be recorded in a court register.

Investigations by HMCS staff has identified examples of a small number of magistrates courts failing to follow the correct procedures. In particular HMCS has identified examples of fees not being charged to local authorities for issuing proceedings and some examples of a failure at Salford magistrates court to enter the results of applications for liability orders on the court register. More seriously two magistrates courts, Rochdale and Salford permitted the local authorities to issue summonses requiring attendance at court without the authorisation of the court.

22 Oct 2009 : Column 76WS
This was a clear procedural failing and was immediately stopped when it came to light. Individuals and the magistrates concerned in subsequent hearing cases would not have been aware of this irregularity.

In all such cases individuals would have had ample opportunity to attend court if they wished to challenge the liability to have the non-payment enforced against them. However they would not have been aware that the summons had not been properly issued. Had the summonses been correctly issued, there is no reason to think the consequences would have been any different in practice. Individuals should pay their council tax and this House would expect non-payment to be properly enforced.

Given the paucity of information available it is not practicable to identify the individuals concerned. The issues identified in Rochdale and Salford have been fully investigated and I am satisfied that correct procedures are now in place. A national check was carried out that revealed no similar practices and all courts have been reminded of the importance of following the correct procedures.

I'm sure that Bridget Prentice at the time must have got a rollicking for bringing this up, as the council tax hearings were not magistrate court hearing, they would have not been covered by any HMCTS & CPR rules. Notice the last sentence in the last paragraph which states, **"A national check was carried out that revealed no similar practices and all courts have been reminded of the importance of following the correct procedures."**

Source
http://www.publications.parliament.uk/pa/cm200809/cmhansrd/cm091022/wmstext/91022m0003.html

So my next step now was to write to the new Secretary of State for Justice:

Dear Elizabeth,

In 2009 the then Parliamentary Under-Secretary of State for Justice Bridget Prentice, addressed the house, on the investigation by HMCS staff on the magistrates' courts failing to follow the correct procedures.
http://www.publications.parliament.uk/pa/cm200809/cmhansrd/cm091022/wmstext/91022m0003.htm

Seven years on, and nothing has changed, in fact things have got worse going on Bridget Prentice's statement in 2009, "HMCS staff has identified examples of a SMALL number of magistrates courts failing to follow the correct procedures.

Magistrates courts are still permitting the local authorities to issue summonses requiring attendance at court without the authorisation of the court.
It seems councils are issuing their own liability orders.
Councils are using electronic signatures on liability orders of persons no long in that position of authority.
Magistrates courts are issuing liability orders without court seals, no printed name below signature.
Magistrates court keeping no record of council tax hearing. Anyone enquiring at the magistrates court concerning a council tax summons or liability order is told to contact the council as the court do not keep records.
I draw your attention to:

SIGNATURE OF DOCUMENTS BY MECHANICAL MEANS
https://www.justice.gov.uk/courts/procedure-rules/civil/rules/part05/pd_part05a#1

STAMPING OR SEALING COURT DOCUMENTS 29.7
https://www.justice.gov.uk/courts/procedure-rules/family/parts/part_29

Tell me how can anyone summonsed to a court hearing get a fair hearing, when the magistrates and council have this cosy relationship?

I look forward to receiving your reply in due course.

Yours sincerely,

Paul Patterson.

Well Elizabeth Truss pasted this on to HM Courts & Tribunals Service | Customer Investigations Team | Customer Directorate 10th Floor (10.34) | 102 Petty France | London | SW1H 9AJ who replied with the following:

Our ref: CW/Nov16 17 November 2016

Dear Mr Patterson

Thank you for your email of 22 October addressed to Elizabeth Truss as Secretary of State

for Justice. I have been asked to reply on behalf of HM Courts & Tribunals Service.

I realise you are concerned about the

enforcement of council tax arrears. It may help if I

explain the basis on which summons are sent out. The Local Authority must apply to the court

for a summons to be issued and, if the court gives approval, they print and issue the

summons on behalf of the court. The Council Tax (Administration and Enforcement)

Regulations 1992 govern this process and limit the powers of the magistrates when

considering an application.

The local authority can draw their own liability orders once these have been granted by the

court and it is for the local authority to ensure that their authorised signatory is valid. There is

no requirement for a wet signature, printed name or seal.

The court does keep a list of the cases once the liability order has been made, however, all case paper work is managed by the applicant and as such queries should be referred back to the applicant/local authority.

The two links which you have included in your email do not apply to civil process in the magistrates' court.

You may wish to seek independent advice about these matters. Citizens Advice provides free, confidential and impartial advice on a range of matters. You could also contact Civil Legal

Advice on their telephone helpline on 0345 345 4345 or find more about the service they

provide at www.gov.uk/civil-legal-advice.

Yours sincerely,

Christine Worsley

Customer Investigations Team

So here we are told that these two rules don't apply to civil procedures in magistrates court.

SIGNATURE OF DOCUMENTS BY MECHANICAL MEANS
https://www.justice.gov.uk/courts/procedure-rules/civil/rules/part05/pd_part05a#1

STAMPING OR SEALING COURT DOCUMENTS
29.7
https://www.justice.gov.uk/courts/procedure-rules/family/parts/part_29

But surely The Magistrates' Courts Rules 1981 must apply which states:

Summons

Form of Summons

98. -(1) A summons shall be signed by the justice issuing it or state his name and be authenticated by the signature of the clerk of magistrates court.
Source:
http://www.legislation.gov.uk/uksi/1981/552/pdfs/uksi_19810552_en.pdf

The fact is nothing applies and there are no rules as these hearing are non HMCTS.

"A rule that is secret cannot be a law" – maxim of law.

The whole procedure, from summons, liability order to Committal to Prison is done completely under a 'Civil Jurisdiction'. Council tax committal hearings in magistrates' courts seem to be conducted under King's Privy Council poor law jurisdiction, illegal and unlawful.

CHAPTER 6

LOCAL GOVERNMENT ACT 1888

http://www.legislation.gov.uk/ukpga/1888/41/pdfs/ukpga_18880041_en.pdf

Powers of County Council.

3. There shall be transferred to the council of each county

on and after the appointed day, the administrative business of the

justices of the county in quarter sessions assembled, that is to

say, all business done by the quarter sessions or any committee appointed by the quarter sessions, in respect of the several matters

following, namely,-

(i.) The making, assessing, and levying of county, police,

hundred,, and all rates, and the application and expenditure.

This Act was revoked in 1971 and it seems that the magistrates' court and council are using this act unlawfully.

It's said the magistrates can only commit a person to prison for willful refusal or culpable neglect, well I don't know what they'll put me under, as my conscience is stopping me from giving any money to a corporation that invests in arms companies. If you are given an order that you think is immoral, you should not carry that order out. You are responsible for your own actions.

Lord Justice Kennedy stated in R. v. Wolverhampton Magistrates' Court, ex

parte Mould [1992] RA 309:

"...the power to commit to prison which is to be found in reg. 41 is plainly intended to be used as a weapon to extract payment rather than to punish .

Mr Justice MacPherson stated in R. v. the Alfreton Magistrates ex parte Darren Gratton (25 November 1993), "... Community charge liability should only be visited with prison (if I may use that shorthand expression) if there is no other way in which the money can be extracted. Prison is not to be used as a big stick or primarily as punishment but as a means of extracting the liability."

CHAPTER 7

MINISTRY OF JUSTICE

This is my latest letter to Ministry of Justice, reply well over due. Sent on 11th November 2016 by law they should have replied by 12th November 2016.

Dear Ministry of Justice,

Can you please confirm the following:

1. On 28th May 2013 committal hearings were abolished in magistrates' courts as part of wider measures to speed up justice and improve efficiencies in the justice system. As a result, cases are now sent straight to the Crown Court as soon as it is clear the matter is serious enough, rather than having to await a committal hearing. Committal hearings were abolished for indictable only cases in 2001. Does this apply to council tax committal hearings?

2. Council tax committal hearing in magistrates courts are conducted under King's privy council poor law jurisdiction.

3. CPR rules don't apply in council tax committal hearings in a magistrates court. The hearings are NON - HMCTS hearing.

4. If council tax hearing in magistrate courts are NON HMCTS procedures, what Jurisdiction do the hearings come under?

5. A liability order issued by magistrates court for council tax, can be set out in a format which the court deems satisfactory - but it will need to include certain basic information such as the name of the person against whom it was made, when it was made and in what amount. It should specify the court which made the order, but does not require a court seal.

The formal order is made by the court, at a hearing in a courtroom open to the public, but the general practice around the country is for the local authority to produce the order after the court has made it. Can you explain why this order from the court doesn't need a court seal. Also can it be explained why there is no printed name under the signature.

6. Are the magistrates courts required to keep records of council tax hearing in their courts from the summons to the committal hearing.

Yours faithfully,

PAUL PATTERSON

Ministry of Justice Reply

Finally on 30/12/2016 I received reply to the above, notice how they don't answer my questions:

Thank you for your email, which has been passed to the team to respond.

The relevant legislation is the Council Tax (Administration and Enforcement) Regulations 1992. The Regulations can be found here - http://www.legislation.gov.uk/uksi/1992/... .

The Council may apply to the Magistrates' Court for a warrant committing a person for non-payment of council tax to prison. The Council will only take this step when other efforts have failed and when an attempt to levy distress has failed.

The relevant legislation is Regulation 47 Council Tax (Administration and Enforcement) Regulations 1992

(http://www.legislation.gov.uk/uksi/1992/... and

Section 82 Magistrates' Courts Act 1980

(http://www.legislation.gov.uk/ukpga/1980...

Before issuing a warrant of commitment, the Court must hold a means enquiry with the person present in Court. A warrant will only be issued if the court is satisfied that the failure to pay is the result of wilful refusal or culpable neglect. The maximum period of imprisonment is 90 days.

Provided the summons specifies the position of the issuing authority (i.e. whether it was a magistrate, Justices' Clerk or legal adviser who issued it), there is no requirement to have a printed name.

There is no statute which authorises (or prevents) a council preparing a summons on the court's behalf. Under section 51 of the Magistrates' Court Act 1980 (http://www.legislation.gov.uk/ukpga/1980..., a person can apply to the Magistrates' Court for a summons. If it is granted, it is customary that the person applying drafts their own summons, which in the case of Council Tax is the Local Authority.

The process of printing and posting of the summons (the issue of which has first been authorised / approved by a magistrate or legal adviser) can be completed by the complainant. It is necessary to distinguish between issuing a summons and the printing and serving of such summons. Only a court can issue a summons, therefore no statute exists allowing Local Authorities to issue summons. The printing and serving (i.e. posting or otherwise delivering) of the summons is customarily done by the complainant.

Thanks

Civil & Family

Court and Tribunals Development Directorate | HMCTS |

Its clear that HMCTS and the council don't want the public to know that these council tax hearing are not held under HMCTS &

CPR. They are nothing more than council hearings held in a HMCTS building. If so, the summons and liability orders hold no authority of the court, they are not court orders. If anything, they are Courts of quarter sessions...poor law jurisdiction - debtor's prisons unlawful & illegal.

The Magistrates' Courts Rules 1981 *contradict the above response in paragraph 4.*

Summons

Form of Summons

98. -(1) A SUMMONS SHALL BE SIGNED BY THE JUSTICE ISSUING IT OR STATE HIS NAME AND BE AUTHENTICATED BY THE SIGNATURE OF THE CLERK OF MAGISTRATES COURT.

CHAPTER 8

CORNWALL COUNCIL'S ENFORCEMENT AGENTS POLICY

Enforcement agents must comply with this policy at all times whilst carrying out their duties. Enforcement agents employed by the Council to undertake specific tasks are required to ensure that they, their employees, contractors and agents comply with this
Code at all times. All enforcement agents must carry:
Photo identification (ID) from the enforcement Agent Company. – This must be
shown to all customers at first contact and on each subsequent visit;
Their enforcement agent certificate. - This must show to all customers at first contact and on each subsequent visit.

Written authorisation to act on behalf of the Council must also be carried. –

This must be produced on request. Enforcement agents must act within the law at all times and observe all health and safety requirements in carrying out enforcement. Enforcement agents must not discriminate on any grounds including those of age, disability, ethnicity, gender, race, religion or sexual orientation that is likely to make the Council liable or potentially liable to a claim under the EqualityAct 2010.

Enforcement agents must carry out their duties in a professional, calm and dignified manner at all times and adopt a polite and respectful attitude toward debtors and other persons they make contact with in the course of their duties. Enforcement agents must be aware that they are agents for the Council and should act accordingly. As agents for the Council, enforcement agents will, from time to time, be called upon to liaise between customers and Council. Enforcement agents must not misrepresent their powers, qualifications, capacities, experience or abilities.

Enforcement agents will maintain an acceptable standard of dress consistent with the provision of a professional service. Enforcement agents should, so far as it is practical, avoid disclosing the purpose of their visit to anyone other than the debtor. All information obtained during the administration and enforcement of warrants must be treated as confidential.

Enforcement agents should provide clear and prompt information to customers and where appropriate, to the Council. If it is found that the customer is residing in a refuge or safe house the enforcement agent will cease collection and inform the Council.

The first thing people MUST do is lose all fear of these Enforcement Agents.

Read these words again, 'Written authorisation to act on behalf of the Council must also be carried.'

For council tax these Enforcement Agents have NO authority from the court.

'Enforcement agents must act within the law at all times.' How laughable, when the magistrates and council are acting so unlawful in their council tax recovery actions.

Here is another one, **"Enforcement agents must not misrepresent their powers, qualifications, capacities, experience or**

abilities." Yet every letter we receive from them states **'I SHALL REMOVE YOUR GOODS FOR SALE AT PUBLIC AUCTION EVEN IN YOUR ABSENCE.'**
Rossendales are clearing committing fraud under the Fraud Act 2006
Fraud by false representation
(1)A person is in breach of this section if he—
(a)dishonestly makes a false representation, and
(b)intends, by making the representation—
(i)to make a gain for himself or another, or
(ii)to cause loss to another or to expose another to a risk of loss.
(2)A representation is false if—
(a)it is untrue or misleading, and
(b)the person making it knows that it is, or might be, untrue or misleading.

Not only are Rossendales committing fraud under the Fraud Act 2006, but the council and magistrates court are by (2)A representation is false if—
(a) It is untrue or misleading, and
(b) The person making it knows that it is, or might be, untrue or misleading.

After ignoring the council's letter informing me of the liability order and how I should pay it, after some weeks I received a letter from Enforcement Agents Rossendales. The letter stated that I had to contact them to make arrangements make payment, otherwise they would visit my premises and remove goods. So I set to and printed out a notice of Removal of Implied Rights and pinned it to the front entrance.

CHAPTER 9

REMOVAL OF IMPLIED RIGHTS

A debtor can remove right of implied access by displaying a notice at the entrance, Lambert v Roberts [1981] 72 Cr App R 223.

Placing such a notice is akin to a closed door but it also prevents a bailiff entering the garden or driveway, Knox v Anderton [1983] Crim LR 115 or R. v Leroy Roberts [2003] EWCA Crim 2753

A person (from 2014 onwards - without a warrant of control) having been told to leave is now under a duty to withdraw from the property with all due reasonable speed and failure to do so he is not thereafter acting in the execution of his duty and becomes a trespasser with any subsequent levy made being invalid and attracts a liability under a claim for damages, Morris v Beardmore [1980] 71 Cr App 256.

A certificated bailiff has only his debt collector hat on without a true warrant of control. No bailiff will have a court warrant of control for council tax. Here is a good site to download all the information for dealing with bailiffs:
http://www.dealingwithbailiffs.co.uk/caselaw.html

To all it concern WARNING ***NOTICE***

to anyone having business/visiting PL13 1QW
NOTICE TO AGENT IS NOTICE TO PRINCIPAL AND NOTICE TO PRINCIPAL IS NOTICE TO AGENT APPLIES
NO TRESPASS

NOTICE REMOVAL OF IMPLIED RIGHT OF ACCESS

You are advised to read the following notice thoroughly and carefully. It is
a lawful notice. It informs you. It means what it says. I hereby give notice that the implied right of access to the property known as PL13 1QW and surrounding areas, has been removed, along with all associated property including, but not limited to, any

private conveyance in respect of the following:
1) ANY employee, principal, agent, third party or representative or any other person acting on behalf of any CORPORATE BODY (i.e. Company) how so ever named and,
2) 2) ANY POLICE OFFICER who is acting for the CORPORATE POLICE and NOT acting as expressed in the Oath of Office of all POLICE men and women, that is as Public Servants, upon your Oath of Office to serve "with fairness, integrity, diligence and impartiality, upholding fundamental human rights and according equal respect to all people; and that I will, to the best of my power, cause the peace to be kept and preserved and prevent all offences against people and property"

COMMON LAW JURISDICTION APPLIES EXCLUSIVELY

Please also take notice that this country is a Common Law jurisdiction and any transgression of this notice will be dealt with according to Common Law. Any and all access to the above mentioned properties shall be by strict invitation only and shall be subject to terms and conditions, available by written request.

We do not have, and have never had, a contract. And any permission that you believe you may have from me is hereby withdrawn. If you believe that you have power of attorney to act on my behalf you are hereby fired, and any consent that you believe you may have, tacit or otherwise, is hereby withdrawn. If you feel so inclined as to enforce statutes as a consequence of this matter I will report your conduct to ALL relevant bodies and will pursue Proof of Claim in affidavit form, under your full commercial liability and under the penalty of perjury. You are deemed to have been served this notice with immediate effect. There will be a charge of £4,950.00 for any incursion what so ever.

In sincerity and honour, without ill-will, frivolity, or vexation
Without any admission of any liability whosoever, and with all Indefeasible Rights reserved.
Errors & Omissions Excepted.

Some weeks after getting the first letter from Rossendales I was waking up the path when I noticed half hanging out of the letterbox was the Rossendales notice. That really bugged me, as I had been waiting in for days for them to call with camera at the ready. Anyway, I phoned the mobile number on the noticed.

"Hello, is that Mr. Bills?"

MY COUNCIL TAX STANCE

"Yes" was the reply, I thought Bills you're havin' me on.

I informed him that I have notice of implied rights on the premises. He stated that he had not notice the notice on the fence. He was very pleasant, he even advised me to put more notices up so they can be seen clearly, and he was 'an extremely obliging fellow.'

He said that Rossendales had told their bailiffs to ignore these removes of implied right notices. He stated the case Thornton v Rossendales Bailiffs...Removal of Implied Right of Access. I informed him that only a warrant of control trumps a ROIR, which the bailiffs will never have for council tax. Anyway Mr. Bills said that he would not call again while the notice is displayed.

Mr. Bills, I thought, I'll look him up on Certificated Bailiff Register, and there he was.
https://certificatedbailiffs.justice.gov.uk/

Well, some weeks pasted, on this afternoon of 19th July 2016 the cat had been asleep on the back of the chair when its ears pricked up. I shot to the front door opening it to the sight of the back of a figure briskly walkin' away. The image that came to mind was of the famous bigfoot video, looking over his shoulder I got,

"I'm leaving, I know you have notice up. I have right to just deliver letter and leave."

I followed him out to his vehicle and had a good chinwag for some forty minutes. I didn't need to but explained why I was withholding my council tax. A Mr. Holden, another decent fellow I thought, wondering when I was going to meet a pumped up steroid taking bailiff. So still haven't got any mug shots. Taking notice from letterbox, in red ink **'ENFORCEMENT AGENT FINAL NOTICE. TAKE NOTICE THAT UNLESS FULL PAYMENT IS MADE IMMEADIATLY I SHALL REMOVE YOUR GOODS FOR SALE AT PUBLIC AUCTION EVEN IN YOUR ABSENCE.'** Once again Rossendales committing fraud under the Fraud Act 2006.

It must have been another couple of weeks before I received a letter from Rossendals this one threatening committal. This is for a court to decide, not an Enforcement Agency. It's a decision for the Council to attempt a prosecution, and it is for them to inform me of any committal proceeding. This is a Misrepresentation of Powers and is punishable by law under The Fraud Act 2006.

At the end of October 2016 received by post headed; Notice of Required Financial Information, stating that I must complete the form and return within 14 days of date on letter. So I thought it was now time to write to Rossendales informing them of the email I received from the magistrates court stating that there were no order against me name:

Notice To Rossendales

It has been confirmed by the court in writing, I have no liability orders in my name PAUL PATTERSON. If Rossendales carry on harassing me by post or visits I will be taking action against the individuals contacting me and their company directors. I draw your attention to County Courts Act 1984 Section 135 & Protection from Harassment Act 1997 Section 2

Legal Notice To Rossendales

I feel the need to point out to you the following established facts;
A. That the summons, hearings and orders are 'Non-HMCTS'...there produced, issued and sent by the council.
B. That NO Civil CPR Rules apply in any of the hearings for council tax enforcement. Perhaps you may wish to confirm what rules apply?
C. That the orders are made in BULK – with 'no legal consideration given individually or indeed collectively' to the summons or issue of the orders.
D. That the magistrates court nor HMCTS have NO record of ANY of the orders made in Council Tax Liability matters.

E. That the Court and Court room itself is purely used as a 'Venue' – and that if ALL parties agree; then the proceedings can actually change venue.

F. That the whole procedure, from LO Summons to Committal to Prison / Bankruptcy is done completely under a 'Civil Jurisdiction'.

G. That no Court, no legal advisor, no court officer, HMCTS, MoJ, Council or even the Supreme Court of the UK – can 'clarify & confirm exactly which 'Civil Jurisdiction' applies and these hearings are held and convened under

H. I advise you to read LLOYD and 44 others.

http://caselaw.echr.globe24h.com/0/0/united-kingdom/2003/10/21/lloyd-and-44-others-v-the-united-kingdom-23523-29798-96.shtml

"A rule that is secret cannot be a law" – maxim of law.

I now REQUEST of you and Rossendales to Cease & Desist any further threat of enforcement.

And as the magistrates court nor HMCTS have NO record of ANY of the orders made in Council Tax Liability matters, Rossendales are not protected by The Protection for Harassment Act 1997.

Merry Christmas to one and all...and unfortunately – If Rossendales carry on harassing me by post or visits I will be taking action against the individuals contacting me and their company directors, firstly by way of Commercial Lien.

Paul Patterson.

Rossendales reply to the above letter on 22nd December saying they will investigate my concern and may contact me to gather further information.

"We will ensure that we can answer any queries and address your complaint in full."

NOW IF THE COURTS AND COUNCIL CAN NOT ANSWER MY QESTIONS, I DON'T SEE HOW ROSSENDALES WILL BE ABLE TO.

CHAPTER 10

LETTER TO MY MP SHERYLL MURRAY

6TH December 2016

Dear Sheryll,

I recently received legal advice that paying tax when it is used for the purposes of terrorism or war is a crime(1). So I'm writing to ask you to ask the Attorney General whether this advice is correct and if it is not to verify which clauses in the Statutes exclude tax from the crimes.

The Terrorism Act 2000 stipulates that it is a crime to demand, collect or pay money for the purposes of terrorism. As the definition of terrorism includes the use of explosives that endanger life for a political cause, and the Supreme Court has suggested(2) that this appears to extend to the military activities of HM Government, it is clear to me that if I pay tax while Britain's military forces take lives in Syria or Iraq I commit a serious crime.

The same principles apply to the International Criminal Court Act 2001, which stipulates that a person commits a crime if they aid and abet a war crime, a crime against humanity or genocide. As the definition of aiding and abetting a crime includes the provision of money, and as the intentional bombing and killing of Afghan, Iraqi, Libyan and Syrian nationals fulfills the elements of these crimes (3), it is clear that paying tax is an offense that renders taxpayers liable for prosecution and punishment as accessories to war crimes.

So I face a dilemma. If I pay tax while HM forces use high-explosive weapons to kill people overseas I commit serious crimes under war and terrorism law; but if I refuse to fund war crimes and acts of terrorism and withhold tax I offend against tax law. I am advised that when two laws conflict I must obey the superior criminal law over the lesser civil law. So it seems that I am duty bound to withhold all payments from UK public authorities until the High Court confirms that paying tax for purposes of war or terrorism is not a crime and guarantees

me immunity from prosecution as an accessory to these crimes.
I attach summaries of the relevant law. Please confirm whether or not these facts are true and the interpretations accurate and advise me on my correct course of action.

(1) Sections 15 and 17 of the Terrorism Act 2000; section 51 and 52 International Criminal Court Act 2001.
(2) UK Supreme Court ruling R 'v' Gul UKSC 64 [2013] paragraphs 26 and 28
(3) International Criminal Court Act 2001 (Elements of Crimes) Regulations 2001.

LAW GOVERNING WAR AND THE FUNDING OF WAR
The Charter of the United Nations 1945
1.3 All members shall settle their international disputes by peaceful means in such a manner that international peace, security and justice are not endangered.

1.4 All members shall refrain in their international relations from the threat or use of force against the territorial integrity or political independence of any state…

41. The Security Council may decide what measures not involving the use of armed force are to be employed to give effect to its decisions…
The Judgement of the Nuremberg War Crimes Tribunal 1946 [Extracts]

"War is essentially an evil thing. Its consequences are not confined to the belligerent states alone, but affect the whole world. To initiate a war of aggression therefore, is not only an international crime, it is the supreme international crime differing only from other war crimes in that it contains within itself the accumulated evil of the whole... Those who plan and wage such a war with its inevitable and terrible consequences are committing a crime in so doing... Individuals have international duties which transcend the national obligations of obedience imposed by the individual State... He who violates the laws of war cannot obtain immunity while acting in pursuance of the authority of the State, if the State in authorising action moves outside its competence under international law"
The Nuremberg Principles 1950

VI. The crimes hereinafter set out are punishable as crimes under international law: (a) Crimes against peace; (i) Planning, preparation, initiation or waging of a war of aggression or a war in violation of international treaties, agreements or assurances; (ii) Participation in a common plan or conspiracy for the accomplishment of any of the acts mentioned under (i).

(b) War crimes: Violations of the laws or customs of war which include, but are not limited to, murder, ill-treatment or

deportation to slave-labor or for any other purpose of civilian population of or in occupied territory, murder or ill treatment of prisoners of war, of persons on the seas, killing of hostages, plunder of public or private property, wanton destruction of cities, towns, or villages, or devastation not justified by military necessity.

(c) Crimes against humanity: Murder, extermination, enslavement, deportation and other inhuman acts done against any civilian population, or persecutions on political, racial or religious grounds, when such acts are done or such persecutions are carried on in execution of or in connection with any crime against peace or any war crime. VII. Complicity in the commission of a crime against peace, a war crime, or a crime against humanity as set forth in Principle VI is a crime under international law.
The Rome Statute of the International Criminal Court – summary of article 25.3 (c)

A person, who aids, abets or assists in the commission of a crime of genocide, a crime against humanity or a war crime, including providing the means for its commission, shall be criminally responsible and liable for punishment.

IF TAXPAYERS OBEY THE LAW, NATIONS CAN NEVER WAGE WAR UK

LAW GOVERNING WAR AND THE FUNDING OF WAR

Supreme Court – R 'v' Gul UKSC 64 (2013) – paragraphs 26 and 28 [extracts]
" *action outside the United Kingdom which involves the use of firearms or explosives, resulting in danger to life ... is terrorism ... the definition would ... appear to extend to military or quasi-military activity aimed at bringing down a foreign government, even where that activity is approved (officially or unofficially) by the UK Government.*"
The UN Declaration on Principles of International Law 1970 [UNGA Resolution 2625]

'Every State has the duty to refrain in its international relations from the threat or use of force against the territorial integrity or political independence of any State, or in any other manner inconsistent with the purposes of the United Nations. Such a threat or use of force constitutes a violation of international law and the Charter of the United Nations and shall never be employed as a means of settling international issues.'
'No State or group of States has the right to intervene, directly or indirectly, for any reason whatever, in the internal or external affairs of any other State. Consequently, armed intervention and all other forms of interference or attempted threats against the personality of the State or against its

political, economic and cultural elements, are in violation of international law.'

International Convention for the Suppression of the Financing of Terrorism [summary]
The States Parties to this Convention, deeply concerned about the worldwide escalation of acts of terrorism in all its forms and manifestations have agreed as follows: Any person commits an offence if that person unlawfully and wilfully provides or collects funds knowing that they are to be used to carry out an act intended to cause death or serious bodily injury to a civilian.

The UK Terrorism Act 2000 – summaries:
1. Terrorism is the threat or use of firearms or explosives endangering a person's life for the purpose of advancing a political, religious, racial or ideological cause.

15. A person commits an offense if he asks for, collects or provides money knowing or having reasonable cause to suspect that it may be used for the purposes of terrorism.

17. A person commits an offence if he enters into an arrangement as a result of which money is made available to another for the purposes of terrorism.

The Accessories and Abettors Act 1861
8. Whosoever shall aid, abet, counsel, or procure the commission of any indictable

offence, whether the same be an offence at common law or by virtue of any Act passed or to be passed, shall be liable to be tried, indicted, and punished as a principal offender.

Yours sincerely,
Paul Patterson.

As of today 31st December 2016 no response.

CHAPTER 11

POOR LAW CIVIL JURISDICTION

In 1971 - the Poor Law Civil Jurisdiction was abolished. Then when they brought the rates in around same time more or less they realised that they needed to keep it.
Yet they are still operating council tax under the poor law. They are using a Jurisdiction that was abolished in 1971.

A London barrister commented to me,

"You make a most important point, Paul. The public do not realise what is happening. I have never liked the cosiness between the councils and the courts and publicity is the best way of advertising this bad practice."

It won't be long before I receive my council tax summons for 2017-18 so the letter to the magistrates' court will be:

Hello.
I have been summons to the magistrates' court to a council tax hearing. Therefore, before I consider attending this hearing I request that the court [not the council] confirm the following for me:
1. Is this a judicial or administrative procedure? & IS this a HMCTS court hearing?
2. Do the Civil Procedure Rules apply to the hearing? If not, which rules do apply?
3. Is the courtroom purely being used as a Venue? & if all parties are in agreement – can we change the Venue?
4. If granted will my Liability Order be made on its own; and with full legal consideration?
5. Has the council served a copy on the court a breakdown of their costs – to justify what they are adding to each LO? If not...why not?
6. Will the court hold a record of my L.O. if granted; if so – how can I get a certified copy of it from the court?
7. How much money does HMCTS receive for each L.O. it allows to be issued and is each one of them signed. For the avoidance of any doubt, I want to make my position clear which is that a Court with no disclosed [civil or criminal] jurisdiction; with no rules cannot be a properly convened court hearing under the British Constitution and therefore is neither a court of law nor record.

8. I draw your attention to the following for comment:

*IN THE SUPREME COURT OF JUDICATURE
COURT OF APPEAL (CIVIL DIVISION)
ON APPEAL FROM The Queen's Bench Division
The Administrative Court
Mr Justice Leveson
CO/6498/2003*

"I find it very surprising that the only document with a court stamp (under xiii) is not produced by the court, but is created automatically by the local authority's software, even though the local authority is a party to the proceedings. (The example before us adds, under the court stamp, the words "Justice of the Peace for the area aforesaid (or by order of the Court Clerk of the Court)". The intended significance of these words is not clear to me.) This document apparently is used only for the purpose of confirming to the bailiff that he has power to act. However, for that purpose the rules require no more than "the written authorisation of the authority" (Non-domestic Rating (Collection and Enforcement) (Local Lists) Regulations 1989 r.14(5)). It seems both unnecessary, and wrong in principle, for it to be presented as though it had been stamped by the court. Nothing turns on this point in the present case, and we have not heard any

submissions about it, but it seems to me an aspect of the procedure which merits reconsideration." LORD JUSTICE WALLER'

9. *"(i) The decision of the justices that the applicant had culpably neglected to pay her community charge without having conducted a proper inquiry into her circumstances 'as of the time that the liability became due' was unlawful, see R. v. Leeds Justices ex parte Kennett [1996] RVR 53.*

http://hudoc.echr.coe.int/eng#{"itemid":["001-68421"]}

I await a detailed written response from the court in regards to this matter.
Please ensure a 'stay' is placed upon my case and it is adjourned until the above have been answered.

Well that's it for 2016. Lets see what 2017 brings. There will be another account on me council tax stance in 2017. Anyone with any thoughts or would like to contact me pattopics@aol.com

Printed in Great Britain
by Amazon